The Unprecedented Melodious Words Of Ajee Da Poet

Shelley Fowler

The Unprecedented Melodious Words Of Ajee Da Poet

Copyright (c) 2014 by Shelley Fowler

All rights reserved. Printed in the United States of America.

No part of this book may be used or reproduced in any manner whatsoever

without written permission from the publisher.

ISBN- 13:978-0615999210

ISBN-10:0615999212

Table of Contents

Dedications..1
360 Degrees..3
Abolition..6
Absentee..10
Agape...15
Anesthesia/Stagnation..22
Be...27
Before...30
Beyond All That We Love...32
Blues...33
Body Bags..36
Broken Vessel..39
Brown Paper Bag...43
Can I Have You?..47
Chameleon...51
Dashiki...55
Don't Tell Me..57
Ejaculation...59
Father, Son and Holy Ghost......................................61
Feelin' You...64
Flesh..67
Freedom..73
Ghetto Womb..75
Glory..78
God Sees..81
Haters...83
I Believe..86
I'm Letting Go...88
If I Was a Bird..91
In The Master's Hands, He Holds The Master Plan......93
Institutionalized...95
Interpretation Of a Single Mother.............................99
Isolation Scream Loudest In Solace........................102
It Was In My Darkest Hour That The Most Light Shined

Into My Life...104
Just Cause..107
Liquid Prayers..111
Love..116
Love And Grace We Found In a Hopeless Place.........119
Man Eater..121
Mariposa..124
Mask..129
Mustard Seed...132
My Soul Is Sore...135
Negro...137
Ooh..139
Open The Door...143
Pomegranate Juice..147
Poverty..149
Reason...153
Rut...156
Scarlet Brimstone..159
Scream!..162
Silent Screams...166
Sometimes...169
Soul Cleansing..170
Soul Mate..174
The Battle That's Fought But Never Won......................178
The Excursion in the Bed that Lives Inside My Head 180
The Gift...182
Without...184
Yet I morn...185
Ying To My Yang, If Not, I Don't Want None............188
You Are Great...192
You're Taking Me There...194

Dedications

First and foremost I give thanks to my heavenly Father, my Daddy, my Lord and savior Jesus Christ. For when the world told me no, You told me yes. I love You with everything that is within me. Without You I could do nothing.

To my dear departed mother, Virginia Medley, who was my vessel to bring fourth my life, I thank you for all the sacrifices that you made for me, I love you more than words can express.

To my biggest supporter to date, my daughter Ashantee Fowler, who gave me encouragement when I felt like giving up, I thank you and I love you whole heartily.

To my son Jordan Fowler, I love you with all of my heart.

To my shining star, my grand-baby Milan, who I draw strength from more than she will ever know, I love you Touga.

To my Uncle Junior, I love and thank you for the many trips to Staples.

To Bishop T.D Jakes for the many teaching that I have listened and applied to my life over the years, I thank God for you.

To my dear sister in Christ Katonja Brown, I love you Mama.

To all who have been labeled outcast, downtrodden, the under dog, this book is dedicated to you, you are somebody. To my single mothers holding it down, this one is for you. Hold your heads up and go for your dreams. No more leaving lamps to our children, it's time to let our true light shine, to create and leave legacies for our future generations.

To all who have been supportive of my endeavors, a thousand times, I thank you.

360 Degrees

I have been turned around

Toss to the ground

Bound

Looking for somewhere to place my feet on solid

ground

There was no one to be found

No longer wanting to be a victim of my own foolish

thinking

I'm tired of sinking in the negativity

That I've been drinking

Causing me to be drunk on the lies

My dreams that want to die

So many tears that I have cried

Longing for the sweet by and by

My feet are so heavy in despair

My lungs are so filled with sorrow I can't get enough air

My stress so deep that my thoughts have burned out

patches in my hair

For me there is no hiding place

I have to constantly keep on my game face

All the while I'm seeking grace

In the weakness of my decrepit state

I become irate

At that moment I cried out please

And fall into my knees

A small voice speaks to me

It tells me I have been waiting for you to set it free

So that I could turn your life around

A fresh start

Dear-heart

Only I can bring it back I wanted you to see

How I will do a new thing

Better than it will ever be

360 degrees

Abolition

My ancestors are the first edition of the recognition

Even though it was over four hundred years

We still suffer from the malnutrition

Of this deposition

Some say it's superstition

But I feel it's a cognitive condition

That has us bound

Seek while we yet may be found

It's all so profound

We are still under submission

Of the composition

Of who's superior

And who's inferior

When I turn on the TV

I see no one who resembles me

It's there to cause demolition

To my self esteem

Not wanting me to be heard nor seen

༄

Longing to drown my definition

While they live as phony mathematicians

When it come to me the equation they come up with is

always

Zero

Making them look like the hero

Never wanting me to grow

To stay in the position of expecting to hear no

My knowledge is my ammunition

Making them hot needing

An air condition

Ah

In addition

I can feel the friction

I want off the repetition

Not looking for a Politician

Nor a coalition

To resolve my requisition

It's time to step from behind the mask of the

cosmetician

Into the exhibition of

Oneself

So open your eyes

Realize

Like an electric shock shooting through the body of an

electrician

Or coming face to face

With a fast moving expedition

It's your decision

You can continue believe

Achieve

Succeed

Or eat the lies fed by a fake dietitian

Use your intuition

For me there is no

Opposition

As long as my body is in commission

I will strive for this self-recognition

In my mind

For the premonition of

abolition

Absentee

With the absence of you in my life

I didn't know how to be a mother

Pick a man

Or be a wife

A whole part of me that held no entity

No identity

Of who I really be

You stole that from me

Leaving me to wander in this world

A grown woman but trapped inside a little girl

You never gave me direction

So I opened my heart without using protection

To those who's intentions was to hurt me

To flee

That was their rendition

To leave me in a fetal position

It's your fault that they became my poison

Causing my heart to become frozen

I had no say in my life it was chosen

⁂

I'm the one that has to live with all the rejections

The erections

The disrespect

The neglect

I can't escape the rapes

That play over and over like a never ending cassette tape

Inside my head

So many times I wished that I was dead

But instead I live

As I hold onto rage not wanting to forgive

You get to lay in a quiet grave

While I'm left to fight the slaves

That are trying to hold me down

Spellbound

I walk around wearing a smile

But

Deep inside in bondage to a frown

I hate that you were never around

I wondered what I did for you to hate me so much

Did you not want to feel my touch

Was it my eyes that you despised

Could I have been a surprise

Or was it my gender

That made you surrender

I mean you were the one who chose to plant your seed

Inside of my mother for me to be conceived

Then when I manifest you leave

Now I'm here in the flesh

With a life full of chaos and stress

I want to beat out your selfishness

How could you not have any repentance

For what you did

Dammit

I was your kid

It didn't matter you just went on with your life

Not even knowing nor caring if I was alright

You left me to fight all these demons on my own

Leaving me feeling like my house was never a home

So I fight hard and cut through the bother

And turned it over to my heavenly Father

Who's showing me

That His love is stronger

Than any

Absentee

Agape

No longer do I have room for contemplation

What I need is a demonstration

The manifestation of the word

I need to see it in the flesh

Seeking it through all this mess

Not through the vision of my carnality

But within my spirituality

When I spoke these words

I was under duress

My eyes covered in blindness

Simple mindedness

That I allowed the enemy

To be my remedy

To take my mind under highjack

Not wanting to give it back

See

What I was looking for had already been professed

God had come down

⁓⁓⁓

He was on a quest

Even though He was in the form of a man

He was still God wanting to understand

All that we go though

He did it all for me and you

His only begotten son

Who never hurt

Lied

Or deceived anyone

He was without sin

But took on all of ours

So that in the end we can win

He laid down His life for a friend

A friend

A friend

Oh what a friend we have in Jesus

Even in his name lies

US

So I'm holding up a sign of protest

Against those who question

My righteousness

Doubting my holiness

Laughing saying that

I'm not good enough for God's best

I have to play what I know on repeat

That I'm blessed from the crown of my head

To the soles of my feet

Repeat

I'm blessed from the crown of my head

To the soles of my feet

Even though I'm moaning

In the midst of my groaning

Only heaven truly

Be knowing

Which direction

I'm going

His word is as sharp as a two edge sword

And I'm standing like a solider waiting

To see the salvation of the Lord

He is my strength

Three strand cord

That's not easily broken

Not lies only the truth

He has spoken

Standing in the crossroad

Of my life

Being pulled in the directions

Of what wrong

vs.

What's right

It's not hard to tell

The narrow road leads to heaven

While the broad one leads to hell

Everyone wants to hear from the god that says

Live your life it is well

It's all good everything swell

Do whatever you wanna do

With me you will dwell

The truth of the matter is

If you didn't give up your life

And follow His

Then the pit of fire is where you will live

For eternity

So you have a choice to pick your own journey

The facade is what you see

That which is not visible is reality

Make sure you don't neglect

And do something that you might forever regret

⁕

In my final words I will say to you

Jesus' love is deeper

And wider than any sea

You can you see

That the gift of salvation is free

It is so great

Make no mistake

He didn't perpetrate

He counted up the cost

That all would be lost

If He didn't go to the cross

Let that marinate deep inside

That Jesus loves you so much

That He died

Not just for you

But for

I

Anesthesia/Stagnation

I have been living a life of condemnation

Confined in a drug induced incarceration

Molestation

Of my own lack of motivation

I reach my hand through the feces of damnation

No longer wanting to live without reconciliation

I chose to leave behind the constant beating inside of

my wrist

So that I can get a fix

I'm done living this remix

See

I'm tired of looking in my kid's eyes

Telling them lies

Selling them phony alibis

They recognize

Know all about the compromise

And they despise

What I have become

The same old hum drum

Oh no

―――

Here it comes

The beating on my flesh

It has become so grossest

This is so insane

Waiting again for the rising

Of a vein

I keep feeding my membrane

Just a little dope

Mixed with cocaine

To stop the pain

To set the memories

In a frame

The portrait

In my mind

Yeah

That it

Frozen in time

Until it rears

Its ugly head

The burning bed

But it was me that was on fire

Too young to even require

⊙≋

You were the one with the desire

And you took it out on me

From seventeen to the age of three

I never asked for you to go upside of me

So you see

That this right here is not for recreation

But to block out the humiliation

To quiet the sounds of ejaculation

Fighting off the thoughts of penetration

While you sealed your own reputation

At the cost of me losing my variation

Not only tearing my hymen

It raped me of real men

Never knowing what they were like

Just like Sofia from the Color Purple

All my life I had to fight

Tomorrow is another day

For me to try to break away

But for now I will continue to live with amnesia

And take another taste of that anesthesia

Then crawl back into my cage of isolation

Once again consumed by this pain that has me living in

total

Stagnation

Be

Be you

Be true

To yourself

You are the only you you got

STOP

Reevaluate

Contemplate

Assimilate

Recreate

Your essence

Your opulence

A breath of fresh air

No one else can compare

You are rare

A commodity

Beyond mediocrity

Worth more than your weight in gold

Let the lies unfold

Until it reaches the core

⁓⁕⁓

Of truth

The youth

That we all have inside

Like Maya Angelou

We rise

Don't remove the kinks from your hair but from your

brain

Marcus Garvey

You have seniority

First priority

To your abundance

Life

You know that I am right

Reach higher from within

When you gonna realize that you will never blend in

With the norm

It's not your form

U lar

It's counterfeit

Not legit

Stop the madness

It brings about a sadness

Don't live like you don't have a clue

Time is overdue

To be true

Be you

Before

Before

I was out of the fluid in my mother's womb

They were planning my doom

Before

I yelled out my first cry

And have my tears dried from my eyes

They were planning my demise

Before

I had my first taste of my mother's breast

They had a bullet ready and waiting to shoot me in my

chest

Before

I could even get sick and get well

They had prepared for me a jail cell

Before

I could get the first kiss from my mother's lips

They told me I would be nothing but a crip

Before

I could even get clear vision

They would not call me by my name but a number given

to me in prison

◈

How could the color of my skin be the cause of all this

hardship and pain

I am not even born yet this is all so insane

Beyond All That We Love

Sometimes in life there are things that are so hard to

forgive

To understand

To relive

Some people are taken from our lives like a wave up on

the shore

Going back out to sea never returning the same way no

more

There are things in this life that make no sense

Have no recompense

No understanding of circumstance

There are just some lives that cannot live upon this earth

They have a greater job to do that involves the universe

Their spirits have to soar to and fro

To be guardian angels to those that they never could
before

Blues

Since you left

I don't know

But all I see is in indigo

In my lack of momentum

I was covered in a wave of denim

My broken heart has placed me in slavery

My mind filled with smoke colored in navy

My fight always begins at midnight

Until the broad daylight

In the prison of my room

Is a deafening gloom

Like being alone on Neptune

I'm so unsure

As I look around at everything drenched in azure

The lost of you I want so badly to rebuke

That I puke

I stand and stare at my toilet covered in duke

I'm not willing to conspire

I reach out my hand, longing for help with nails the

color of sapphire

―――

Even though I prayed to die

I look up to the sky

Hoping to get another glimpse of your Baltic eyes

My clothes are wet from aqua tears

Seems as if I have been crying for years

I've toiled

Over the one I saw as royal

You were my strong tower

The one who would grace me with cornflowers

Every taste of your lips withdrew my power

You were so eclectic

Your body electric

In the distance you saw a holt

And chose to revolt

You jump on your colt

The only thing I saw was the waving of your trench coat

dyed in smalt

I couldn't take it so I threw myself in a sea of cobalt

No longer wanting to be seen

I took myself to a place of one constant dream

Where everyday would be a Caribbean

Body Bags

I wonder did the man who invented the body bag

know that black people would be needing them more

than any other race

Did he know the pace

That we would be killing each other off like flies being

swatted on a hot summer's day

With no conscious of foul play

I wonder if he knew that black mothers would be in the

streets crying wild

over the slaughter of their child

And fathers would be raising their hands to the heavens

seeking understanding

Filled with anger wanting to retaliate reprimanding

While black grandparents keep on out livin'

Their dead grandchildren

I wonder if he knew that the dreams of young black children

Would be cut down washed out to shore

No more

I wonder if he knew that the loud long dragging of that thick black zipper

Would seal off the gifts that God placed inside

With no chance for compromise

I wonder if he knew that they would be laid out in morgues by the dozens

Through death becoming distant cousins

I really wonder if knew that the black youths would be murdered at an alarming rate

Through malice

Lack of love

And hate

Are just a few reasons for this state

Too many to name

The problems too great

Like the devastation of a train coming off a track

I wonder why he made the bag black

Broken Vessel

I was ripped from my inner veil

All I could do was wail

As this well known male

Who sails out with no bond

No bail

Or time in jail

I'm the one who is left frail

My mind keeps reliving the time when

He broke through my hymen

Everyday

I'm slowly dyin'

The pain of that night has never left me

I've carried it into my destiny

Perpetrating like I was fly

While all along I was getting high

It was my Novocain

Bringing joy to my membrane

I couldn't get enough cocaine

After a while the white dust

Made me become promiscuous

Allowing me to trust my feelings of lust

Now enjoying the stolen most precious part of me

Giving it away so freely

With each body that I held tight

I pretended that every wrong I was doing was right

With no humility in my abode

My body became a human commode

Can I get a witness

I was just a place that they did their dirty business

Paying me in orgasms

Proud of their mechanisms

I give up

No more men

I'll try lesbianism

None could fill my emptiness

All of it was just a band-aid covering up my madness

Teetering on the verge of insanity

It's so uncanny

No one understands me

Putting me in their judgment box casting their vote

Thinking that they know me 'cause I use dope

Their too afraid to pick up the soap

To wash away their own dirt to reveal what they use to

cope

I will not hide

Be covered

Nor nestled

I will expose that I am human but more than that I'm a

child of God who is a

Broken vessel

Brown Paper Bag

You can't brown paper bag me

White flag me

Tag me

Snag me

Into your ignorance

Not accepting my difference

Wanting me to think that checking a box will cause me

consequences

Of my future expenses

You're looking through the world with rose colored

lenses

You don't control

My body nor my soul

And your feelings towards my skin color

Kissed with the rays from the sun solar

I will not allow the dolor

Of your bipolar thoughts

Needing the center of disease control

To take a stroll

Through my mind

⁕

'Cause

He has made me whole

You

Now you live erratic

Always dramatic

But as for me

My ways are systematic

I live under the law

The one without a flaw

Not the one that you follow that's full of nothing but contraband

Mine it comes from my Maker

My Father

And the motherland

He holds the world in the palm of His hands

He spoke a word causing my obsidian complexion to emerge

No longer having the urge

To create another

My God understood

When He was done with me He said it was good

So when people put you down

Don't allow yourself to be bound

By your race

For not liking the glowing color on your face

Longing to erase you

Even though they try to brake you

Shake you

Or be fake

No matter what it takes

Remember that God doesn't make no mistakes

Even when they wish that you would gag

Hold your head high don't you dare let it drag

You are fearfully and wonderfully made

By your heavenly Father

On you He brags

And

Who doesn't judge your greatness by a

Brown paper bag

Can I Have You?

Can I have you?

There is something that you do to me

I just want you to take me to ecstasy

See

I have never laid eyes on you

And you never laid eyes on me

But it's something about you that can take me from all

the stress and strain

And at the same time you turn my joy into pain

Can I have you?

When I think about all the things we said

All the things that go through my head

Wanting you here laying in my bed

Can I have you?

When I sit and wait for your call

I become frustrated when I don't hear from you at all

It makes me wanna scream

Is this reality

Or a dream

I mean

―――

I can't understand how a man that has never touched my

body has me trembling

Assembling him in mind

Can I have you?

See

Sometimes I think he knows

Even though I try not to let it show

How he makes me feel

Damn

I'm trying to keep it real

When I don't know what to do

I'll go old school

Hop on yahoo

Messenger

You will pop up and say hey

Mmm

That just brightens my day

Can I have you?

In the wee hours of the morning we are doing things

that makes us both feel the vibe

Both our natures rise

I am not surprised

Can I have you?

Sometimes when I awake

I know that what I feel for you is not fake

That we have been somewhere deep within each others minds

We share so many dreams that are genuine

I have felt the touch of you holding my hips

Tasting my lips

Can I have you?

I wonder should I have you in the physical way

Will all of my feelings that I have for you go away

Or should I keep you as my fantasy

And stay away from the reality

Either way

Can I have you?

Chameleon

I'm tired of giving people dominion

Over my opinion

I want to be a declaration

No longer a clone of my past generations

I have inside of me the power to change nations

Moving away from those with minds of degradation

Wanting to commit fornication

Through manipulation

On my reputation

'Cause I'm not down with the majority of the

congregation

Humiliation

Procrastination

This is an abomination

I have chosen emancipation

To contemplation

To live in segregation

Sanctification

Not needing your accreditation

For my interpretation

Of who I am

I don't owe you any documentation

on the

Proclamation

Of my own independence

Me

I am free

I don't have to change

Nor rearrange

My thoughts

Because you are deranged

Within your brain

Avis

Power to the people

Angela Davis

You see me as a threat

Because I can't be kept

In the confinements of your

Four walls of toxic apartheid

Seeing me less than because I menstruate

The truth in me rumbles like a earthquake

It makes you regurgitate

My thoughts are too strong

My name ain't Rodney King

So I'm not trying to get along

Your stomach can only hold deception

Too weak for consecration

Wanting me to live in genocide

The Devil is a lie

You are only pleased when you run lives like you are the

Taliban

You're hating me 'cause I take a stand

You keep livin' with your mind in incarceration

I'm rebellion

A womon

Not a chameleon

Dashiki

Life for me ain't never been easy

To those on the outside looking in might have thought

my home environment was freaky

I wasn't greedy for material things

But for love

Yeah

I was needy

Although the things I did were sleazy

I tried to keep them put away neatly

Hiding them discreetly

The thoughts of my lifestyle routinely

Made me feel queasy

None of my past was measly

But extremely beastly

Everything I had done was carved onto my mind like

graffiti

No longer wanting to be down

I meekly bow out

Like the wind

Breezy

I seek to become a new specie

―※―

The person that use to be sneaky

The one like a wheel

I'm the one that was squeaky

Reintroduce myself to the world

As the new created

Defined young woman

Uniquely

Known as
DASHIKI

Don't Tell Me

You think you know so much

Don't tell me to sit down and shut the hell up

When I'm tryin' to raise my kids on a daily basis

In world full of racist

Tryin' to find myself in an existence that tells me I'm

less than

Not seein' me as a woman

Nor a man

And after the war

That I don't even know what I was fightin' for

Uncle Sam turned his back would not take a stand

Would rather throw me out like garbage in a trash can

When my babies' daddy don't wanna pay child support

Tellin' me to abort

That negro won't even show up for court

When my kids are lookin' at me for somethang to eat

And I gotta hustle to make ends meet

Don't tell me to sit down and shut the hell up

⁓⁓⁓

When you're ridin' around in a Lexus coupe or Bent

And I can't even pay my got damn rent

Lookin' down on me like ya betta

Knowin' deep down inside that I'm the true go getta

The one who can make a dollar outta fifteen cents

And make thangs happen wit little substance

Havin' to fight for everythang along with my common sense

Not to mention even my own independence

So I will continue to stand

Even through the eyes of society I'm labeled corrupt

I will never sit down and shut the hell up

Ejaculation

The force of the shot ejaculates through the chamber.

The smell of burning flesh defecates inside my nostrils.

It entered in the flesh, breaking through the muscle and marrow.

I longed to release myself again, pop!

It feels so good. I close my eyes and take it all in.

One bullet at a time, they find a place to plant themselves.

The cries are not released in ecstasy, but agony.

They are feeling what I feel.

Their facial expressions are mixed with fears and tears.

They make a connection to my soul.

It reaches out to me, then it dies leaving me with my silence sufferings.

I need to ejaculate again.

This time I placed the foreskin of the chamber up to my

temple.

My temple.

My body is a temple.

A temple that is full of evil, I could see in a dark yet dim

corner its longing for love.

My eyes looked down at the body that lies at my feet.

I have changed roles with God.

⸻

Oh, I need to once again release myself.

One last time.

Shot to the head, dead, dead, dead!

Father, Son and Holy Ghost

I no longer want to fight life

But without a choice it has hook up to me like a

husband to a wife

It keeps on fighting me

Punching me until I can no longer see

Pushing me further from the light

Trying to confuse my wrong into a right

It wants to rebuild the walls that I fought to break down

Wanting to rebound

It continued to follow me like my shadow

Like the darkness of a sparrow

Always one step behind or close to my side

Never giving up

No chance of compromise

Every time I felt that the battle was won

It would steal the warmth of the sun

It would come reminding me that it holds the upper

hand

Too many times like trying to count the grains of sand

What I didn't realize

I was trying to fight in my limited strength

My arms didn't have enough length

I had to learn to release my grip and allow the Father to

use His

He was the only one who has the ability to handle all of

my biz

Ness

The war that was raging was not in my flesh

It reach way beyond my consciousness

But flowed in my spirit like water from a faucet

I couldn't win in my carnality

So I had to let God entered within to set me free

With Him reigning I could win

Through the deadliest of my sins

So when I feel there is no hope

And the weight of the world on me is heavier than most

I cry out for help from the Father, Son and Holy Ghost

Feelin' You

What must I do

I'm feelin' you

What can I say

To make you feel this way

I'm feelin' you

Just the thought of you brings me great joy

I'm feelin' you

Sometimes

I feel like your toy

A puppet on a string

Umph

You have that special thing

I'm feelin' you

What am I to do

I'm feelin' you

When I close my eyes I can have you for my very own

⚜

I'm feelin' you

You got me in a zone

I'm feelin' you

It's so funny

You like the honey

And me

I'm sho'nuff the bee

What have you done to me

I'm feelin' you

Can you see I need to feel your taste

Your touch

Is this lust

I'm feelin' you

I wonder if you ever catch me glancin'

I'm feelin' you

I love watchin'

I'm feelin' you

Your body moves like your dancin'

I'm feelin' you

If I had the chance to let my feelin' show

I would open up and let you know

I'm feelin' you

Flesh

This exterior

Can be quite superior

If ones not careful to surrender to the interior

The mind is strong

But the flesh is weak

It can give off the sense that it is meek

But if untamed it will not be discrete

It looks to seek its own selfish desires

And turns good men into liars

It acts like gasoline that is thrown into an already blazing

fire

With its own greed

It will stampede

Mislead

It doesn't care if you are married

Just all long as it has succeed

In getting what is needed

It will cuss

―――

Fuss

And give into lust

Its not worthy of trust

See

Your flesh will put you to the test

Never letting you rest

Causing you stress

It and your mind will fight

And one of them will win whether it's wrong or right

Sometimes flesh can feel like it's on fire

Squirming for what it wants to acquire

There have been times that it has taken over my eyes

I can't even lie

Every part of me tingles

Wanting to intermingle

With what shouldn't be rekindled

It has whispered in my ear

You know you want it

Go on and flaunt it

Don't front on it

Come on take the chance

Their no place for recompense

In this circumstance

Hmm

I lick my lips at the thought of filling my narcissism

Not caring about anything but my egoism

Like cannibalism

I allow it to devour

Not caring about the day nor the hour

I know my decision will make my relationship turn sour

A foundation built on lies

That neither one of us can recognize

Concrete slathered in rejection

Of our imperfections

Searching for direction

On which way to go

Wanting to know

How I ended up in this row

This corridor

Fa sho

It was me wanting more

Taking on what I didn't bargain for

Not satisfied with what was bestowed

I chose to open a closed door

Longing to shut

I could feel the danger deep within my gut

There are no if's

But's

Or maybe's

The only person that I played was me

I presented you with a present of mistrust

Wrapped in a bow of disgust

And paper that glisten in shame

How could I allow this to be my claim to fame

A tarnished name

I have no one to blame

It started with a melancholy touch

That trickled into a tiny crush

That exploded the flood gates

It was too late

Like Sodom and Gomorrah

In the thrush

Of their adulterated

Immoral

Diabolical

Conduct

So I was the one who got an F on my test

And gave into the weakest side of me

My

Flesh

Freedom

Can you hear it ringin'

I hear it singin'

Freedom

Opened up showin' me the kingdom

It's here that heaven

That number seven

Completion

Freedom

I'm runnin' towards the sun

The pain of my past is done

I have finally become one

With myself

No longer on the shelf

I know my wealth

It has not come to me with the use of medication

But through prayer

Meditation

Supplication

Even degradation

And separation

Have laid the foundation

Of who I am

A young woman

Who had to learn to stand

Right in the middle of God's unchangin' hand

Freedom

I don't know where to start

⚜

All I know is that it has taken up residents

Deep down inside of my heart

Freedom

Ghetto Womb

It like bending down seeing my reflection in a crystal

clear stream

You are more beautiful than I could have ever dream

The miracle of you was placed inside of my poison

womb

In the beginning

I felt sorry that you were being developed in that

decrepit tomb

Then love forced its way in

Making room for itself to bloom

Never caring about the poverty and the stench of gloom

All that was ever known deep down in there was pain

Death

Heartache

And despair

I wondered how anyone would be able to survive in there

Unaware in the stillness of the night I would send you a little prayer

My dear darling

Without saying a word you sing sweet like a starling

Sending the melodies of your movements straight to my heart

Knowing that we would never be apart

You have swept the cobwebs of hate from the shackles of my mind

You caused me to no longer be blind

You taught me the true meaning about mankind

And that I don't have to let my pass define

Me

See

You knew when the time was right to force your way out

You kept coming without fear

Or doubt

You fought through the falsetto

Of a womb that knew nothing but the bondage

Of the ghetto

Glory

I know He loves me

I know that He cares

He knows everything about me

Right down to the number of my hairs

He's all up in my business

Concerned about my affairs

If anyone dares

To attempt to cause me to fall

My Daddy will deliver me from them all

When you tell those I gotta stop her

My Daddy said

That no weapon formed against me shall prosper

Those that thought I was done

Putting me on a shelve

But God

Told me to be like David

And encourage myself

When all around me is so dark that I can't even muster

up a smile

Not knowing what to do

God said after you have suffered for a little while

I will establish you

On my journey though the desert

He showed me everyone one of my frenemies

While catching all the hell

He prepares a table for me in the presence of my

enemies

When it's all say so done

My Daddy will leave them shaking their heads

Telling everyone the story

Not knowing it was never about me

But about God getting

His glory

God Sees

Does God see

All of my misery and pain

Does God see

All of my fear and all of the shame

Does God see

All the times that I have failed

Does God see

All the times that I have wailed

Does God see

All the doors that were closed in my face

Because of the color of my skin

And my race

Does God see

All the times when people did not understand what I

say

Does God see

Every time I fall on my knees to pray

Does God know

My every trial and tribulation

And does He know the right time for celebration

God says

That without putting me into the fire

I would not be able to handle what He desires

God knows

That the world I will never be able to please

And look to Him for all of my needs

Even though it's hard

I do believe

That God sees

Haters

Stimulators

Aggravators

Manipulators

These are some of the factors that they hold

No goals

Straight up cold

Perpetrate a roll

Trying to sliver into your mold

When they think that they know the facts

They will smile in your face

While stabbing you in your back

So busy worrying about you

That they can't keep their lives on track

You worked hard to reach your achievement

All the while they wishing for your bereavement

See

They don't realize

Their being used for you to reach the prize

While they were running their mouths about you on the

phone

※

They became your stepping stone

Their evil conversations of your lateness

Pushes you into greatness

While they were pulling the rug from under your feet

You became a masterpiece

They huddle together and laughed to see you fall

Now they look confused to see you standing tall

They said that you would never get outta this

Not realizing that you have a God that said you are to

legit to quit

So take a bow and give a standing ovation

To the ones who tried to end you with their schemes of

temptation

It's a celebration

To the motivators

That we call

Haters

I Believe

I am a woman who longs for better days

No longer wanting to be a slave to my thoughts

And negative ways

Wanting to feel the true meaning of embrace

Not just from a man

But through the touching of my face

Knowing that I have the power within to change nations

To bring down strongholds

That have been kept captive for so many generations

I am an army of one that holds a sword of positivity

With one swing of my hand

I can destroy all soldiers of negativity

A force to be reckoned with

I know that God has placed in me so many gifts

Not sitting around waiting for someone to tell me that I

can achieve

'Cause I already know the impossible

Is never impossible 'cause

I believe

I'm Letting Go

I'm letting go

Of all past pain

Things that have me hurting

Trying to drive me insane

Those who ridiculed me

Beating me down

Not letting me stand my ground

Those who wanted to rape me of my soul

Not letting me have any control

Those who treated me like

I was nothing more than mortal

Those who laughed and rebuttal

Those who felt my existence

Was taking up space

Not wanting me to be a part of the human race

Those who spit in my face

Hoping that the wetness would make my life erase

In haste

Told me that I was a disgrace

My mind replaced

All those lies

Those silly alibis

With the truth

They hated me 'cause they could see the fruit

That I produce

That's why they wanted to cut me down

They didn't want it to abound

But my feet have been planted on solid ground

See

I know now that without all of this torture

And pain

My life would have never been the same

It has brought me full circle

And created in me a miracle

It has taught me how to love

It has come from God up above

Through all the darkness

Stress and craziness

My life accumulates

My heart still glows

And illuminates
Even if they wanted to stop me
It's too late
To seal the fate
'Cause I already know
That will continue to grow
Because I'm letting go

If I Was a Bird

If I was a bird I wouldn't be worried about how I would

eat

What I would wear nor where I would live

'Cause I would know that God gives

He would supply all of my needs

Without a thought of a seed

That humans have for greed

Even with wings He would keep me under His

Though love that needs no quiz

He would orchestrate my dances with the wind

And grin

At the flapping of my wings

He would sing

Loving me like a fruit tree

Proud of what He had created in me

Knowing that He could do anything

But I am not a bird

And I have no wings

So I cannot fly

⁂

No matter how hard I try

Yet and still His eye is on the

sparrow

More so on me who's been created in His shadow

Setting me free yet

He's always watching over me

In The Master's Hands, He Holds The Master Plan

You took a life that was full of no hope

That was filled to the brim in darkness

Through it all I thought I was alone

You had me covered in Your love

When I could no longer walk on my own

You elevated me in the strength of Your arms

The foundation of who I am was created before the

earth was formed

Even though I waded in the muck and the mire of life

You were there to lift me out of my gunk

A lump of filthy clay in Your mighty hands

You placed me on Your potters wheel in the universe

Turn by turn clumps of the old me began to fall away

My life was spinning

I had no control

All the tears that I shed You used to reshape me

You began to smooth the roughness out of me

While You're not done with me yet

And there are times I can't see my way clear

※

I know that I'm safe

In the Master's hands

Who holds the master plan

Institutionalized

Its been so long that I've lived in this penitentiary

For what seemed like more than a century

It was so abrupt

That I was corrupt

To the way I was living

Locking myself up

My Armageddon begun

When I hid in this dungeon

Within

It was the only peace I had from all of my decrepit sins

See

It was just too many stories

That I couldn't let them escape the reformatory

Of my heart

No chance for a new beginning

No way for a fresh start

My generational appointed adversary

Kept me in solitary

As he became the beneficiary

⁂

To the whisperers of my pain

I had nothing to lose

And most certainly nothing to gain

What could have been a house of correction

Had to become walls of rejection

Living in a barricade

People have thrown me a lot of shade

Never even knowing that my stockade

Was the closest thing to lemonade

To quench my deteriorated thirst

Only for things to become much worst

There is no sledge hammer

That can breakthrough this slammer

Of my no longer existence life

Never will I be a wife

A mother

Or have another lover

The darkness fills my soul

Like a black hole

There's no other point

Just me

And my thoughts are confined in this joint

I'm coming to my demise

Me

Umph

I'm not surprised

This is to be expected when you live your life being

Institutionalized

Interpretation Of a Single Mother

The life of a single mother is not any easy task

See

You always have to put yourself last

Make sure the kids have something to eat

Clothes on their backs

And shoes on their feet

Always making sure that they look neat

Even if what your wearing is incomplete

Being a single mother is hard

You got to protect ya seeds from the crazies

That will be tryin' to enter ya yard

A single mother always has to be on her grind

She has to work hard to keep her joy

And her peace of mind

She doesn't have time for much fun

'Cause she knows in the lives of her kids that she is the

one

The only one

That they got

―――

To lean and depend on

If mama's gone

There's no more home

The hats she wears are always changing

She does it all

Never once complaining

After she tucks her children into bed

She will finally get to lay down

And rest her head

She thanks God for providing their daily bread

Even though the angels in heaven are above her

There no one more stronger

Than a single mother

Isolation Scream Loudest In Solace

My scream are loudest in the isolation of my mind

My solace has made me blind

A madwoman draped in intelligence

Smiling through my negligence

So many emotions have taken up residence

Fighting to kick them out but they are persistence

I'm covered in lace

Smothered by its taste

No longer wanting to emulate

But longing to regulate

All of my sorrow

Seeking a brighter tomorrow

Lord

It's so dark in here

The whispers of your light I hear

The somber voice of you saying have no fear

I'm so close to you that I'm catching everyone of your

tears

⁌≋⁍

I'm washing you crystal clear

I have given you the greatest love

And that's the shedding of my blood

Take me by my hands

Of mercy and grace

And together we're walking out this solace place

It Was In My Darkest Hour That The Most Light Shined Into My Life

Living with no form of understanding my wrongs from

my rights

I took a seat in the darkness of my plights

I was in a war and many fights

Not knowing my days from my nights

This felt like a cinema

As I wondered if I had some form of schizophrenia

The solace of my breathing is all that could be heard

The flow of my tears

That clung onto me for so many years

My silent words that only God could hear

He spoke back to me telling me

I'm here and have no fear

I can feel Him rocking me in the wallow of my sorrow

Reassuring me that if I hold on He would give me a brighter tomorrow

Just when I thought everything was going to be alright

I was tossed into the darkest of night

I was hanging on the ledge

Praying with all my might 'cause one more step I would topple off the edge

So close that everything should be lost

But Jesus

He counted up the cost

That is when a ray of sunlight shined through my brokenness

That was the warmth of God telling me to rest

He came to take away my stress

Beaming down on me His conformation

And His righteousness

Letting me know that I had indeed passed my test

Just Cause

Just cause you are saved doesn't mean you don't struggle

with

Fornication

Humiliation

Masturbation

Molestation

But through Christ there is

Restoration

Manifestation

Rejuvenation

He paid it all so there is no more

Condemnation

So open up your heart to the celebration

'Cause through prayer and supplication

God is transforming us into a nation

Under one foundation

Of consecration

It's time for jubilation

Keep your hands to the plow

Don't wait till the battle is over shout now

'Cause with God as your friend you gonna win

Pen to paper

Like ink to a tree

Jesus paid it all for us to be free

So be blind no more

Use your eyes as a sword

Just like Moses said

You shall see the salvation of the Lord

His rod and His staff they comfort me

It's so powerful that it parted the Red Sea

God gave Esther

The strength

To stop the fester

Of murder that would have killed off the chosen people

If this would have happened there would have been no

sequel

The rest of us would have been in danger

There would be no king of kings lying in a manger

No cross for Jesus to hang from

No hope for the gentiles to be won

Just death without a resting place

A fall that wouldn't have any grace

God so far off in the distance

With no chance of repentance

No more existence

It's not flawed

Everything God does

Is for a

Just cause

Liquid Prayers

Sometimes when I fall on my knees to pray

No words come out yet I have so much to say

My vision is viewed through the color gray

With a small dimmer of light

'Cause you

You will never leave and always stay

Even living in dismay

My life in disarray

Your mercies are beautiful everyday

I seek you with contemplation

Yet

I think about people not knowing you in their situations

The single mother living stressed

She ashamed of the way her children are dressed

Her babies daddy is doing two term bids

While she has no food in the fridge

To feed her kids

Her baby sucking on her breast full of nothing but air

With salty tears rolling down her face she unable to bear

⁂

Or the father feeling less than a man

Who has not even a penny in his hand

Longing to be a provider

He feels like an outsider

Trying to see through the blurriness of his tears

He's been looking for work for over three years

Not having any money in his hand

He comes up with a master plan

His mind began to erupt

He decides to become corrupt

Stick'em up

With no hope of getting any jobs

He robs

What about the professional dancer

Struck down with cancer

She felt the lumps

But thought it was just a case of the mumps

Her body became covered in goose bumps

When her hair fell out in clumps

The man that she loved didn't want a chick

That was sick

So like a banana peel he split

A child being bullied in school

'Cause he wasn't cool

He tried to fit in

Yet they continued to be cruel

And played him for the ultimate fool

Not willing to put up with anymore BS

He changed his style of dress

Then added a touch of finesse

Everyone became so impressed

By his progress

Now they considered him a success

Their friendship they were all willing to deposit

Not knowing that under his shirt was a gun from his

father's closet

Feeling like Blade

He slowly slipped on his shades

He shot the backs

Of those who had no idea he was taking Prozac

In a flash

He killed more than half of his class

Even his English teacher Mr. Bill Blass

Felt the backlash

'Cause he over heard him too many times calling him an

ass

―――

All of this just makes me stop and stare

Like watching the sparks that come from a flare

So much pain hiding behind

What are considered liquid prayers

Love

I can smell it, is savor is so sweet.

I can feel it, its touch warms my virtue.

I can hear it flowing through the billows of my heart.

I wanted it, but I hated it.

I ran from it, but I searched for it.

I cried for it, and screamed at it.

It intertwined itself around me.

Wrapping me up all in it.

It was too right not to be wrong.

So I fought it.

When it left me,

I was a wreck without it.

When I had it, it kept me warm in the winter.

It shaded me in the summer.

Shield me from the wind and the rain.

Now, I'm naked.

Vulnerable to the elements of life, that want me to

wither away.

My heart has become a stone.

⚜

No longer beating to the rhythms of flesh.

I am blind.

Patting my way through the darkness.

The windows of my soul are black.

Will it ever come back to me?

Will it ever look for me as it once did?

I was drowning in the sea of my closed heart.

I was going under for the last time, when love grabbed

me.

Lifting me out, embracing me in my own fortress of

despair.

Love will creep in between the steel of a maximum security prison.

Into the night of a homeless shelter.

Into the filthiness of a crack house.

It will kiss the wounds of a dope addicts' tracks.

And shine a pond the isolated, destitute and the outcast.

It will raise up the underdog and dance with the downtrodden.

Love can heal the sin sick soul.

Rock its pain away like a new born baby safe and snug in its arms.

Love will keep you even if you don't want to be kept.

It never gives up on you.

It believes in you.

It loves you.

Love And Grace We Found In a Hopeless Place

I saw your face

In a hopeless place

In your eyes I saw something that couldn't be replaced

In a hopeless place

You laced my lips with yours that was sweet like

honeysuckle to the taste

In a hopeless place

How could two people from a different race

Living in minds of an enclosed space

Find so much love

In a hopeless place

The light of your love illuminated warmth through the

cockles of my darken heart

Giving me a fresh start

The space in me that has always been desolate

You came and colored with the beauty of your love

Tessellate

A hopeless place

Time will never erase the grace of love we found

In a hopeless place

Man Eater

She rises late in the evening

Money is on her mind

She looks in the mirror

Knowing she oh so fine

She catches a glimpse of herself from behind

Knowing that she's a bonafide dime

She gets ready for her nights pray

Laughing out loud

She already knows what they are going to say

Many of them lust

Some want her trust

But deep down they were all so disgust

Ing

She would laugh when those of them would offer her a

ring

Some had a plan

Desiring to take her hand

In marriage

Wanted her to push a baby carriage

They longed to feel like a rebel

So bad that they would sell their souls to the Devil

For one touch

One taste

One cut

⁂

Hoping she could relieve them from their rut

Not seeing her for what she really was

A slut

She don't want them

Only their Benjamins

She was once a good girl

That lived in a good world

She had the best and never had a want

No bootleg for her

Naw

She didn't front

From the cars to the clothes

Prada

Gucci

Fendi

Louis Vuitton

She was the female reflection of a don
She had it all in droves
Her daddy even brought her a Rolls

Nothing but the best until she wanted to take a test drive
She went to a place that she didn't know how to survive
She took a trip in the passenger seat
Speeding down the road called defeat
On the drug train
And going insane
She couldn't control it
She just didn't know how to quit
She was buggin'
From all that druggin'
Now she keeps chasing after the pipe dream

Things aren't always as they seem
Somewhere in the back of her mind she think that she is still a diva

But the reality is that the drugs have become the real man-eater

Mariposa

Mariposa

Sammy Sosa

Arroz con pollo with black beans

Seen

I ain't no puta

I keeps my panties clean

I have a dream

I want to be like a moonbeam

No

More like jelly beans

Minus the negro ones

When will I ever overcome

I'm Malcolm X

By any means necessary

Down with being a revolutionary

Just not for the commissary

I'm so voluntary

Hmm

Who am I kidding

I'm pretty much sedentary

I wonder why the hell does my Uncle Charlie

Walk around thinkin' that he is Bob Marley

Always tryin' to sing

Thinkin' he's the life of the party

Wantin' everyone to listen to what he says

But me

I just stare at his bald head

No signs of dreads

He drinks Red Stripe beer sayin'

Mi no no mi dear

So sincere

He's so queer

Not in a gay kinda way

Just strange you know what I'm tryin' to say

If you don't then that's a personal problem

Okay

Let me keep goin' before I forget what I wrote

'Cause sometimes my thoughts to me are so dope

If I shoot every evil in my view with my AK47

Will that still give me the keys to unlock heaven

If I repent

Sometimes I think that my mind is so bent

Will they give me a monument or a holiday

Mold me outta clay

Naw

What for I ain't gonna hold my breath for that day

From the cradle without the grave

I'm free

Yet

I still live like a slave

In a new kinda way

The constitution and the declaration of independence

Really adds up to dollars and cents

If you don't got it your on the road without recompense

See

There is no seniority when your livin' in poverty

You are a blank canvas invisible to the naked eyes

No one knows you in the midst of your demise

They smile in your face

Then roll their eyes

Pushing you to the corner of the world

So this goes out to every

Man

Woman

Boy

And girl

Spread your wings

And run like a testarossa

༺༻

Fly

Fly

Fly

Mariposa!

Mask

On a brisk day in September

I realized that have lived behind the mask

For as long as I can remember

That I have never allowed the world to know who I

really am

Like a million dollar bill

My life has been a scam

Feeling that the world has always had a

misunderstanding of me

Not being able to express the real me

That I long to be

Alone

Rejected

Neglected

Wanting to live my life unprotected

When will this society get past the outer shell of my existence

Even in my resistance

I peek out into the distance

And look deep within where all true beauty dwells

There is so much love inside of me

But I hid behind the mask, too afraid to let anyone see

⁓⁂⁓

When will I truly be able to set it free

No longer wanting to be my worst enemy

Removing from my memories life's past tragedies

Before judging me look at your own insecurities'

So much hypocrisy

No more generosity for the human soul

Tell me why have we become so cold

All of these situations trying to kill me

Messing with my mentality

Plotting my demise

When will they realize

That I wear the mask that the world has given me

But that doesn't mean I won't continue to fight behind it

Until I am total free

Mustard Seed

Through the blurriness of my tears

I fight my heart that longs to be filled with fear

I open my ears

You draw me near

To hear you praying

Even when I don't know all that you are saying

When I look all around me things become distractions

Causing me untrusting reactions

Trying to work things out from my own actions

Ignoring the fraction

That you are the only one that can make me whole

Knowing everything about me

To the depths of my very soul

Allowing the one who takes a stroll

From to and fro

Who only came and stole

For a moment

My discernment

One

Two

Three

Just like the prodigal son I came to me

Myself and I

I

I

Threw my hands up to the sky

Not understanding why

I continue to try to serve the most high

Even in my desert places that are bone dry

A small flame in my heart

That hasn't depart

Ed

From me

I cannot deny

That God will supply

All of my needs

From His riches in His glories

He's taking inventories

On how much I believe

In my need

If I have faith the size of a mustard seed

If I don't fold

And continue to hold

No good thing will He withhold

And

I will come forth as pure gold

My Soul Is Sore

When I was inside my mother's core

My soul is sore

Before I could bore

My soul is sore

From the first time I adore

My soul is sore

When they brought me through the door

My soul is sore

At four

My soul is sore

Every eyewitness of uproar

My soul is sore

The fists that landed in the midst of my mother's war

My soul is sore

Screams I heard begging for no more

My soul is sore

Hatred fills my every pore

My soul is sore

The heroin filled needles that I saw

That rested on velour

My soul is sore

Born carnivorous

Yet

I still wonder what's in store

It will never take away that

My soul is sore

Negro

Negro

Moreno

Black

Those are the words that many represent as lack

Of knowledge

Wisdom

And understanding

Always reprimanding

Why would they think that my rebellin'

Is caused by my melanin

No

It's due to all that I have witness is jellin'

In my mind

I see

But yet they want me to stay blind

To what's going on in these last days and times

So much poverty

Hatred

And crimes

Tell me where's the reason

Wanting to understand the rhymes
Look at me
I have been kissed by the sun
I wear the identity of the first chosen one
So the next time you want to call me
Negro
Moreno
Black
To my face or behind my back
Just remember this fact
That I am a beautiful strong woman
And yes
I am BLACK

Ooh

Ooh

It's something about that man

He's like that Haagen Dazs butter pecan

All natural

Smooth and sweet

From the crown of his head to the soles of his feet

When he touches me I get a chill

He knows how to make my time stand still

He is so complete

He's discrete

He's solid as concrete

Damn

He even has nice feet

Ooh

It's something about that man

When he's walking towards me

It's in slow motion

He's so loving

And full of devotion

―

When he makes love to me

He takes his time

Slow

Dutty whine

No R. Kelly involved

No rush to just bump and grind

First he always makes love to my mind

Ambitious

Delicious

Lord

He's infectious

He's so fine

One of a kind

He loves being in my world

He treats me like a Nubian queen

Not a little girl

He so secure within himself

He shares his wealth

What more can I say about this man

He understands

He takes life by the hand

He can be gentle as a dove

But he will fight for his love

⁌※⁌

He takes care of all my needs

Physically

Mentally

And emotionally

He even protects my unborn seeds

He may not be known near or far

But in my life

I couldn't live without his repertoire

He will always be my shining star

Open The Door

One day I was looking out the door

I noticed a woman I hadn't ever seen before

She was in a dress

It was free flowing

Moving like it had a mind of its own

Not knowing

She was smiling holding the hem of her dress

So carefree without any repress

She was singing

Spinning

Dancing

She was romancing

Herself

It was like she found her true wealth

She was free

Wanting everyone to see

She had so much peace within

That it was blinding

To those who couldn't comprehend

I could see the glow of God shining on her face

She was in a place

Of contentment

No resentment

Just free to let all the love flow

She let her mind grow

Oh

I could see she was free from her woe

Drenched in illumination it spilled outside

I was so surprised

It was so bright

No more darkness of night

She let go of the fright

That lingered inside of her

She knew that she was more than a conqueror

With Christ that dwells within

He traded her a crown

For her sin

She was bold

No longer cold

No more full of hate

God sealed her fate

So blessed

No longer stressed

Free from being depressed

When I looked closer at the woman

I couldn't understand

What I had seen

This whole scenario changed from red to green

When that woman turned around she was me

So I opened the door and set my own self free

Pomegranate Juice

Rolling in a sea of love

My lungs are filled with passion

The deepest of crimson

Its sexiness rippled its waves of ecstasy

Across the nakedness of my cappuccino

With a splash of mocha skin tone

Intertwined me in your flavor

Let's make history through our divine essence

Of unadulterated penetration

Until transparency unveils the purity

Of who we are

Let's stop time until the only existence is

Eternity

Where the force of gravity is removed

And our minds are free flowing

Everything else had disintegrated

Your love permeates every part

Of my creation

Leaving me fortified

Cultivating me in every climax of rapture

We're never famished

Always voluminous

Saturate me in your cognitive

Perception

Implode me with your dialogue

We are encased in each others bosoms

Drink

Adore

Poverty

Poverty goes deeper than the limitations of depth to

ones pockets

Like a socket

It plugs into the vertex

Causing the mind to become complex

The equilibrium

Becomes numb

Making those it affects feel the need to succumb

To not having none

The lack is causing those to figure out how to get some

Of that cash

Dividends

Moola

Guape

You go get a glock

Start a business selling rock

Not knowing that inside you are well stocked

You need to change what you feed

And plant seeds of positive prosperity

―――

You have no clue

That God said that your gifts would make room for you

With God you can't fail

You are the head and not the tail

No longer do you have to live in grief

Don't you know that you are above and not beneath

Stop treating your heavenly Father like a foreigner

He wants to make you the lender and not the borrower

You don't have to get hook up with a click

To make you feel legit

God already made a place for you to sit

'Cause the blessings of the Lord maketh rich and add no

sorrow to it

Poverty is more than the lack of

Cash

Cars

And clothes

It's the lack of wholeness in every area

Especially your soul

The way to end poverty and break its chains

Is to give your life over to the One who reigns

Your blessings will fall like rain

And those who want to become the show stopper

Will not succeed

'cause no weapon formed against you will be able to

prosper

So step out of the majority

Reach for a level of seniority

And become the one who stomps out the spirit of

Poverty

Reason

Is there a reason why you always put me down

Why you never wanted to see me happy

Always trying to make me frown

Maybe you knew all the gifts I had inside of me

And was afraid I would figure out all of your insecurities

You always tried to break me

And underestimated what I could possibly be

Every time you told me I was nothing

God

Told me I was something

When you tried to kill me

God

Filled me

What did I do that was so wrong

I wasn't asked to be born

Yet you treat me like I'm no one

When you decide to let the sunshine within in your heart

Then we can make a fresh start

―――

But until then we must part

No more beating and slapping me to the floor

No more telling me that I'm nothing but a whore

See

I know that I'm so much more

Then what you are giving me credit for

You are the one who's living in fear

'Cause I know my purpose for being here

With that being said

I will open the window to my heart

To let all this pain depart

To allow the breeze of God to wipe away my tears

That I have been crying for so many years

So

I will asked God to have mercy on your soul

I'm leaving you

Breaking free

And no longer under your control

Rut

There is no need to be slangin'

Or bangin'

They are so elementary

Yet those things have become a normal part of the

twenty first century

What we need is to be livin'

Lovin'

Learnin'

Growin'

So that through our lives the youth will be knowin'

The truth

How can we live in a society

That is deceived by commodities

This is the hypocrisy of humanity

That has raped us and become profanity

Where some have more and most have less

This is what causes the stress

Leavin' many feelin' under duress

Because of so much selfishness

Lawlessness

That has manifest

Why wouldn't one retaliate in self defense

Against the forces that wage war within

This has become a sin

That has no beginning and very little hope for no end

We turns our heads like we don't see

That the youth are dyin' inside

Not just physically

But emotionally

Mentally

And spiritually

So

The next time you see a young man with his pants

under his butt

Or a young girl with a big belly

That you know ain't a gut

Ask yourself did you play a part

In this sociological

Genocide

Immoral

rut

Scarlet Brimstone

Fire engine red

Blaring inside my head

Boiling like hot lava in my spirit

Spittin' out fire flames and not even fearin' it

Love is the essence of you

This has everything to do with them

Two

My thoughts are filled with rage

I long to turn the page

But unable to 'cause of the blaze

I'm caught up in a maze

No longer wanting them to faze me

My fury can bring forth a repercussion

It beats like the sound of a percussion

Pressure cooking at its peak before explosion

Causing my erosion

There's is so much truth that it can hold its own weight

That it's a thin line between love and hate

'Cause in between love

Love was created

And hate between us was formulated

It spread its disease to the deep part of my cranium

Damn

I loved how I'm just hatin' him

And him

I would stab both of you and watch you bleed

But my greed

For the need

Of my seed

And my creed won't allow my selfishness to feed

So I fight hard for my child

Not wanting how I feel to be cloned

Not wanting him to be enraged

Like scarlet brimstone

Scream!

Don't look at me like you never wanted to scream.

Maybe 'cause you have not fulfilled a dream.

Or your lack of having enough cream.

Dollar

Dollar

Dollar bill ya!

I long to rise

Yet I fall.

Scream!

I said

scream!

Yeah!

Scream out for all of those that have raped you!

All that have forsaken you!

All that have mistreated you!

All that have tried to defeat you!

All who have lied on you!

All who have denied you!

Those who have pushed you away!

⊚∞

Those who have lead you astray!

Those who spit in your face!

Those who hate your race!

Those who tried to take control!

Those who wanted to rip out your very soul!

Those who were bold enough to hate the uniqueness of

your mold!

Scream!

Out the insanity!

Scream!

Out the profanity!

Scream!

Out no longer wanting to be the majority!

Scream!

Out for those living in poverty!

Scream!

Out for the dying babies!

Scream!

For the government full of if's

And's

But's,

Or maybes!

When you open your mouth didn't you know

It was the roaring of the vocal cords!

That brought down the walls of Jericho!

You have the power to bend beams!

To rip negativity at the seams!

Don't just sit there!

Open up your mouth!

And

Scream!

Silent Screams

No one can hear what I'm going through

It is silent like the fall of the morning dew

It cannot be heard

Longing to be seen

Wondering if my canvas is showing a sheen

Of my silent screams

Will anyone understand what I mean

I'm living behind a smoke screen

That's covered with an unclean

Obscene

Serene

Like gangrene

It can't be wiped away with chlorine

It hides in the hollows of my flesh

Inside my blue jeans

It lacks hygiene

If it had a color it would be yellowish green

Not even a vaccine

༺❀༻

Nor can the pain of it be medicated

By codeine or morphine

By the naked eye it's not foreseen

How could I allow the scheme

To mess up my dreams

Rip what I loved to the seams

Destroying my self esteem

I longed to be redeemed

From my silent screams

They roar the loudest in the darkness

They manifest leaving me breathless

Covering me in its comforter of bleakness

I must confess that all of this stress

Is causing a lacking rest

If I could just get this off my chest

I mean

I want to confess

But it like getting naked in public

It's hard to undress

So I guess on my quest

To fester through all this mess

I'll do my very best

⁂

Not to go to the extreme

To keep a lid on it

As not to let out steam

And try to find peace somewhere in the midst

Of my silent screams

Sometimes

Sometimes in life we breath but can't get enough air

Sometimes we fight against ourselves

Knowing deep down inside that life sometimes is unfair

We shut ourselves off from the world

Trying somehow to remove ourselves from the turmoil

Sometimes we fall from all the pressure

And battle against ourselves beyond measure

Sometimes we wonder when all the pain and lack of understanding will end

Then out of nowhere without notice comes a friend

Someone to take us by the hand

And make us feel like we can live again

They can make all those dark clouds roll away

Letting us know that there is a brighter day

Soul Cleansing

The outer can easily be cleanse

My inner is the filthy lens

I need a gully washing

Sloshing

Of my soul

It's so deep

Dark

And cold

A spot in me where my story is told

I hid in there not wanting the truth to unfold

That's the dirt that can't be seen

It's all in my crevices and in between

I'm holding on to my anger

Hate

Resentment

And pain

Not only in my heart

But in the depths of my brain

༺❦༻

See

They are both connected and one in the same

There are so many I long to blame

Too many to call by name

I'm filthy

Nasty

And carry a stench

A no good wretch

I am

But you chose me to be the apple of your eye

As hard as I may try

Somethings in life never answer the why

It's enough to make the strongest of men cry

I can't lie

You're comforting as a piece of warm sweet potato pie

That's a surprise on the forth of July

Spread my wings and fly

You are the true meaning of ride or die

'Cause you did

For me

And I had nothing to give

Yet all I can do is live

For you

You dug deep down inside of my most inner being

A place I never knew that there could be rejoicing and

singing

You and only you could perform in someone like me

With no hope for a happy ending

A

Soul cleansing

Soul Mate

Where are you

Are you really true

I have been looking for such a long time

To find that one who is sublime

The one who I long to seal my fate

To find my soul mate

I dream about you all the time

I wonder if I'm on your mind

Are you somewhere out there looking for me

Waiting to see

Praying that our paths cross

Hoping that all is not loss

Never trying to erase me from your thoughts

I have a vision

An incision

Of you on my heart

You will be smart

And strong

Never wanting to do me wrong

A loving man

That takes my hand

Telling me that everything will be okay

Never stray

You will stoke my hair and kiss my forehead

While you hold me so tightly in bed

You assure

Allure

Always encouraging

Never discouraging

Me

Of my hopes and dreams

Of things not always being as they seem

You will take care of my needs

Not for greed

Understanding

Gently reprimanding

Sometimes I wonder if you have already come to the

end of your life

Before I had the opportunity in the flesh to become

your wife

Has my love already gone home

Leaving me here to fend for myself

All alone

Are you up there in the sky

If so

Then why

My heart cries at the thought of you not being here

All I ever wanted was you

My dear

My eye sheds a tear

Will I have to wait until I'm called home to see my love

I looked to the heavens up above

If this is the case

Then I will just face

The pain of going on while I wait

To see my soul mate

The Battle That's Fought But Never Won

The battle is not in a far away zone

But in the confines of my home

Where the gun fire is from the blows of a closed fist

With us caught in the cross fire wondering why

We didn't enlist for this

We were thrown in the muck and the mire

Under fire

Of two who live life like they are in distant lands

One is Israel

While the other is Pakistan

And we are the children who throw up our hands

Longing to understand

Wondering how two people who can say I do

But now one says imma kill you

While the other shouts we're through

Even if the white flag of surrender was raised

It would be unrecognizable from the blood

Sweat

and tears it gave

No hope to be saved

The battle has made them both slaves

To the maze

Of the many times they forgave

Only to rekindle the rage

Again

Battling like two men

In a war they engraved on their hearts

Minds

And souls

The two of them never found a way to control

And to think that we would be better than what our eyes

withhold

With the odds stacked up against us coming from the

same mold

So the war rages on

Though the machine guns of their fist and their tongues

Still are used as ammunition to cause the destruction and

rebellion

The Armageddon of their children

The next generation

The Excursion in the Bed that Lives Inside My Head

I will spread the red blanket across the bed.

Place the basket where you lay your head.

Put the wine on the night stand.

Come downstairs, shield your eyes and take your hand.

Guide you to our pleasure play land.

I will sit you so gently on the bed.

The one that lives inside my head.

Kiss your lips and caress with a slight tease.

I will feed you bread, grapes, wine and cheese.

And after I have feed your temple, I aim to please.

Your mind, body and soul.

Letting you have your way with me, being in total control.

And afterwards,

we make that type of love where we can't tell where our bodies begin and end.

How could this be?

Your not even a friend.

This is nothing but pretend.

Inside of my cortex.

We will never have sex.

If I was a Caucasian girl and you found out, I would be turning red.

Loving you is something I will never dread.

I explode.

As I look forward to our next episode.

Our excursion in bed.

That lives inside of my head.

The Gift

Today I receive a call

Not from a stranger but from a friend for no reason at all

See

She is always taking time for healing someone soul

It's just a gift she has not under her control

She is one of a kind made from a special mold

She came to me and left me a gift

That I can hold

Leaving a piece of her heart and soul

Sometimes we feel that the gifts we can see are the greatest gift in our reality

But being able to touch a heart is a gift that comes with no box

Making you feel secure as Fort Knox

She's that type of friend

Someone you can count on to the very end

Giving you an instant face lift

She's a rare commodity

A special gift

Without

Without love I'm like a sheet of paper blowing aimlessly

in the wind

No sense of direction

No start and no end

Just flowing to and fro

Never getting the chance to know

How real love may feel

It's all unequivocal and yet so unreal

When will my life not feel like an empty space

So longing for love and acceptance from the human race

Without this love that I so desire

My soul will never be rekindled and set a fire

Wanting to free myself from all fear and doubt

And to find that love that I no longer can live without

Yet I morn

There is no casket

Yet I morn

There are no flowers

Yet I morn

There are no people all dressed in black

Yet I morn

There is no somber music playing

Yet I morn

There is no preacher floetically saying a eulogy

Yet I morn

There is no body to view

Yet I morn

Just the thought of being without you a death has taken

place

I ache deep down in my soul knowing that our love will

no longer be

As I look in the mirror

My tears are flowing as suddenly as a spring rain shower

I'm dying inside

This pain is more that I can bear

I morn

Will you ever come back to remove this pain from me

I wait patiently

Meanwhile I morn

I wonder if I have made footprints across your mind

Yet I morn

The end has come

It's so hard to except the finalization of our love

The casket of my heart has been lowered

The dirt has been thrown

No longer do I morn

For I too am deceased

Ying To My Yang, If Not, I Don't Want None

If I can't have that type of peanut butter with jelly

That meal so good make you rub your belly

kinda love

If not

I don't want none

A flower needs water and sunlight

A wrong that compliments a right

kinda love

If not

I don't want none

He gotta be the baseball to my bat

That scarf to a hat

A cat that chases after a rat

Yeah

Down like that

'Cause that's where its at

If not

I don't want none

⁓✺⁓

As a champagne bottle has a cork

As dinner is eaten with a fork

And a Muslim don't consume no pork

Yeah

That kinda love

If not

I don't want none

Like laces go with a shoe

That's how I be needin' you

But if you not feelin' me like I'm feelin' you

I don't want none

Like a lighter to a cigarette

And a fisherman's need for a net

He must someone I'd never forget

If not

I don't want none

I mean that ice cream to a cone

The dial tone on a phone

A dog's lust for a bone

Kinda love

If not

I don't want none

He must be able to keep me in a zone

Always rising to the top of my dome

Kinda love

If not

I don't want none

My body is not a playground

I'm not looking to be played for fun

We have to be each others number one

Kinda love

If not

Whoa

Y'all already know

I don't want none

You Are Great

People will judge you and tell you lies

Wanting to decompose you like a dead caucus covered

with flies

They will tell you are not pretty enough

Not witty enough

You're too fat

You're too black

These things are not facts

But what they want to do is creep up inside of you

Longing to hold you back

These are decisions

That cause serious contradictions

To fill you with grief and disbelief of who you really are

A star

The reality is that they want to walk in your shade

They see what you are made

Of

They want to be above

Desire your ability to love

They sit in groups discussing your life

Never seeing the wrong or the right
Inside of them
Yet they can condemn
You
For being true
See
You outshine any negative energy

You are an entity
That flows miraculously through life
While they consume trouble
And belch up strife
If you don't have a clue
There will never be another you
So let them sit back and amalgamate
Conjure up lies
And formulate hate
Make no mistake
You are great

You're Taking Me There

You're taking me where I don't want to go

In this time and space I'm learning to grow

Like a blood clot you're stopping my flow

You're taking me to a place where there is no grace

You gonna make me put you in a place

Where the sun will no longer shine upon ya face

Yet another casualty to the human race

You drew the straw that gonna seal your fate

It's unorthodox

But you made your bed become a pine box

Tick tock

Tick tock

Do you hear the ticking of your time clock

I long to hear you scream and shout

Before I take you out

You have caused this tragedy

For messing with me and my family

☙

So you have taken me where I never wanted to go again

To reach out and pick up my long lost friend

I can't pretend

The hour has come for your end

You're taken me there

Got me going buck wild

New jack city style

I know you was hoping for a chance

A maybe

But no

It's over

Rockabye baby

Shelley Fowler, is a native of Hackensack, New Jersey. She resides there with her daughter Ashantee Fowler, son Jordan Fowler, grand daughter Milan Fowler, and Brooklyn the family's Yorkie.

www.ingramcontent.com/pod-product-compliance
Lightning Source LLC
LaVergne TN
LVHW051116080426
835510LV00018B/2078